T0359977

TEARS IN MY BREAD

TEARS IN MY BREAD

Maria Papageorgiou Foroudi

ARCADIA

© 2020 Maria Papageorgiou Foroudi

First published 2020 by Arcadia
the general books' imprint of
Australian Scholarly Publishing Pty Ltd

7 Lt Lothian St Nth, North Melbourne, Vic 3051
Tel: 03 9329 6963
enquiry@scholarly.info / www.scholarly.info

ISBN 978-1-925984-92-7

All Rights Reserved

Cover design: Amelia Walker

Contents

The Womb

I wondered how changed you would be
By the knife and needle

They brought you back home
Patched up like a quiet broken doll
The stitches running like track

Do they take a piece of your soul
When they take the womb?
Clamping its neck
With cold metal
Lifeless
Like a beautiful scarlet bird

Red and bloody it must have hung:
Shot with cautery and
Captured between forceps
And the triumphant hand of the
Surgeon

Once a month I recall you blossoming;
A warm blush and the heat of your
Honesty would send us all
Scurrying
As if the blood was daring to escape through
Your eyes and cheeks and
Mouth
Like a red soldier

And I thought:
This is what it means to be a woman

For once a month
Like it or not
You became who you really must be –
Undeterred by edict
And convention
And guided by your heart and mind:
Or perhaps the cry of mothers
And grandmothers
Locked deep in the cage of sex

Canopic

It's a Sunday ritual
To come back to the old house
Of childhood
Its walls bubbled and broken
Like a burst plaster chrysalis

The corn is slumped in the garden
As bald as priests:
Their gold hair burnt by summer's breath
The silky bandages singed and
Their yellow teeth as scattered
As a mummy's

This flaking hut still
Holds my lungs and stomach:
I clasp my breath
And my guts crease when I enter
The dark hall

Walls as still as jackals
Their borders lined with the kohl of judgement

Autumn

Our eyes are on the purging tree
Which unleafs in the autumn winds
Like a body about to be washed:

Its bony fingers tapping on the hospital window
Like the knock of an impatient knuckle

It's easier to look out
Rather than at each other

His arms seem so much skinnier than the last visit;
His face a little more sallow
And mysterious cords drain
The yellow sap of his bladder

My son stands amongst the elms in the park below
His legs kicking a football as red
As Easter
As I hold my father
His flimsy white sheets fluttering
To the ground

The Sewing Machine

I spent my weekends watching her foot press the pedal
Of the old Singer sewing machine:
Fascinated by the silver tooth
Which bit the wool and cotton under her finger
Watching dresses and trousers
Pieced together from the threaded
Mess

It was a few years later that I began to
Lose the stitch
Of my brow and arms and
Mouth
Falling apart with a rip here and there
Arms joined to torso with loose threads
As if the air and sun and night slowly
Were removing the tacking
Which joined me to my skin
My clothes becoming long and dark
Like a winding sheet
Hiding still under cloth

And I began to wonder:
Perhaps strong feet
And hands can piece together
A flooded eye or bent back

If they moved as fast as a dressmaker's hand
They could make a shirt of spring or dress of armour

With flashes of silver and steel
The balance wheel spun forward
Like an axe

Garden

The wild lilies grew with a flourish
In our garden
As white as bandages
Amongst blades
Burnished by sun

He would spend the morning among them:
Gently tapping the soil on its brown shoulder
Like an old friend
Careful not to disturb
Heads as pristine
As a nurse's cap

And flicking the purple braids of the chinese spinach
Over the timber stake which spread under
The quince he would stop and admire
His lot

Lifting my face from the books
I would see his sharp secateur hover above the lemon tree's
Malignant bulge
His face angled toward the house
And I would watch the shears spit out what had caused offence

I turned my eye quickly back to the page:
Keen to plough my own fields
Of page and paper

Restless

My grandmother's eyes rest in my hand tonight:
A buckled black and white photo cradled in my palm

Her young face is melancholy and wan
Carrying the burden of the field and home
And her thin braid reminds me of a noose:
It is the winter of '33
And a son is placing first footsteps
Under her ribs

His feet are destined to walk out of the schoolroom
At nine
Wrapped in pigskin and frozen by snow:
Kicked out by SS uniforms and boots as polished as knives

Fleeing his village
With a broken vinyl suitcase
Made heavy with dreams
A couple of drachmas tucked in a shoe
Dripping with the waters of the Suez

The sickle of the village was abandoned for
The punch card of Melbourne factories:
Restless feet which danced in share houses
To bouzouki cries
And sighs and stares
Tracing pain with each step
And never finding home

Cinema 1968

Fleeing Melbourne factories on hot Friday afternoons
Where she had spent the day dressing
Peanut and almond chocolates
In shiny red

They would dive into art deco cinemas
Filled with salty popcorn
And colour posters
Their neon signs winking compulsively at rushing crowds

Mother waited in the shadows for
Nargis and Elvis as if they were long-lost friends:
Saris and guitars in an unlikely embrace
While her own pale blue shift drooped with sweat

Screens of black and white
Flickered with dance
And the plaintive songs of
Bollywood
Which made her cry and laugh in equal measure:
Though she didn't understand a word
A photo of her mother sat tucked in her bag

My father hid in the flickering
Night-blue shadows next to her:
Lemonade-drunk and
Snoring

Chennai 2006

The taxi wriggled like a beautiful woman
Through the Chennai traffic
As eager to be seen
As I am to watch:
A metallic parade
With stops and starts as decreed
By the driver's impatient foot

And on the side of the freeway
A tent flap flutters like an eyelash
And a mirror hangs inside

A young man stands before it –
His back to the road
Oblivious
Sensuously combing nutmeg dark hair
And straightening his shirt
Staring into the mirror like Narcissus

Preparing himself, perhaps,
For an evening of love when the shadows fell:
Negotiated and purchased like the finest spice
By the side of that busy road

Fruit Picking

I will pick some fruit today
Swinging plastic buckets among fat vines
Answering cicadas with my
Boots
I might try a raspberry or strawberry
Hot as pie
Sugar red running from bruised
Skins

The raspberries hang dizzy with syrup
From the blazing sun;
As bumpy and red as nipples
Waiting to feed our open mouths

My greedy fingers grip a thorn

It's only fair
We both bleed

Blue Eyes

I saw hundreds of crystal eyes
Hang from a tree in Cappadocia
Floating on its arms like bracelets:
Bobbing blue caiques
Or gaze-filled plums wearing eyebrows of leaf

And I wondered
How did the blue eye become evil?

When it is the sea

And vein

And sky

Perfect blue eyes lined and coloured
With sapphire ink:
Whoever pronounced you evil

Was afraid of life itself

Market

At the market
Only the unblemished will do
Squeezing avocado and plums with
Eyes and fingers
My ears overwhelmed
By stall-holder's overtures

How delicate the splayed rabbit is;
Hanging pink and glistening
Reclining on couches of parsley

The hunt ends with a pause of evaluation:
'That one' I say
Shifting my empty bag
From armpit to hand and licking my lips

While a man follows me
Much too close behind

Stage

I've worn out my heels
Making noise
And scratches
On this glass stage

When in fact the most profound moments
Were found in stillness:

And the quiet of love and death

Both fell dumb in my arms
After the wave of cry fell:
And I held them

Stroked them in sleep
My silent lip bleeding with bite

Grape

Some wine spilled on the tablecloth tonight
Staining it as red as late summer sun

Cutting the air with drops dripping on my hands
Red question marks on my white
Sterile shirt

How is it:
That a tiny grape can make us dance
And love
And cry

Surely it is no accident
That it is the colour of a cut vein:
For it first had to lose its skin in crush
And trampled underfoot it fermented
Solitary in the darkness of the cellar
And became blood

Words

The words curdled on my lip
Like old milk
Difficult as it was to describe the wonder
Of swelling
As an almond tree in spring

My hand had left the pen
To help trace an 'o' and 'a'
Taking his tiny hand to the paper

Delivering his first words
I smiled and stood with pride:

Like a barren midwife
Grasping for the kick and beat of my own lost syllables
That tapped lightly on the side of my head
Like the tick of a distant clock
Echoes and flutters
In the dark of duty

Pillar

If it were not for my need to be
A pillar
Salt of the earth
I would have lived an honest life

Yet if my pale hand was to read my
Mind
Tracing the wild braille
It would fall upon it like a guillotine
In disgust

And lucky for that strike;
How perfect it all stays
As neat as an accountant's fringe

Let those messy dreams
Remain stillborn and unkicking
Let their promise be mangled
By the coat hanger of duty

Lot's Wife
Keep your eyes
On the perfect path ahead

Tomb

There was a time
When their bed became a tomb:

Their bodies stretched and still
On sheets wound white and
Flecked with salt
Unable to face eyes which were filled with ending

In the dark
Their faces were buried in contemplation
Under still masks
Painted with expression
And tables and chairs
Creeds and flowerless vases lay
Bundled to the side of that sealed room
To use some other day
Some other time
Perhaps in their afterlife:

And through the small window

Autumn stole through like a robber

The Visit

Knee deep in shadows of tomato and
Nectarine it was the slow rumble of the bus
That had my mother scrambling from the garden
To her feet

Moving to the kitchen to count the silver coins
And collect me from play;
We walked from the silent house
Which slept in fog and shadow
To the crunch of the ticket
Punched by the driver with
His tiny silver oar

She seemed to linger longer than usual
Outside the factories where she had worked;
On Commercial Road
And Chapel Street

Her eyes feeling and watching
The air like a cat
Moving her hands nervously across the broad
Canvas bag
As if it were an ouija board

And as if by magic they would appear
Pale and smiling and gliding towards us:
Old friends made over pasta packs
And biscuit production lines

Pinching and kissing my cheeks
Practiced as they were picking and packing
In those factories
Those shrewd eyes weeding out damaged goods

I would listen to the farewells
As the bus edged closer;
And they slowly started to fade
As I burned my fingers on oily dim sims
Steaming in brown paper bags
Words and cries ringing through chimney stacks

The coins dropped
And the driver smiled ready for our return
Ferrying us over rivers of dome and church
To the Tartarus of home

Kindergarten

In between the pastel paints and easels
And the chipped tea sets
Of kindergarten
We served and sipped the air
Heavy with the expectation of duty:
Primed for a life of service in our pretty dresses
And bows

And the toilet walls were mysteriously short
Low enough to see who stood
And who sat:
Daring to hover like a boy
I spoiled my dress and earned
A teacher's disapproving glance

Perhaps I deserved to lose that lock of hair:
Scalped by a boy in a polyester cape
His arms akimbo on the plastic castle
Above me
Holding a trophy of pretty strands

Necklace

She once told me:

'Adornments are for the fallen'

And yet I made her heat the needle
That pierced my ear
Making her
Crookedly jab the unwilling skin

The diamond stuck fast
Like a shiny Venus
And stayed there for years

Years later at the gift-shop
I found a necklace of a thousand orange discs
Which dripped like yolks
Or foreign suns
Around my neck

I will be sure to wear it
When I visit her next

Mykonos

It was a thousand mornings ago
That I escaped the snore-smacked walls
Where the children slept
Sitting by the jasmine-licked
Bannister of that Mykonian
House cat-like in the dawn

Tied to the steep Cycladic
Walls I watched the last shoeless revellers
Stumbling in beer-steeped wraps
Toward unmade beds:
Their empty bottles
Roughly swept by village women with disapproving
Stares

The Aegean waves nearby moaned loudly for the morning
As they had for centuries:
Slapping the shore with salty hands
Awakening the fisherman's boat
And the eye of the island priest

Ladder

I search the dusty boughs
For the finest fruit;
Always a little out of reach
Those gold-spined pears
Dripping with the nectar
Of fact and law

But somehow my foot never did fit
On those ladder steps of fine wood;
Perhaps it was too wide and
Broad like a peasant's

They yearn for earth:
To sink into veins of olive tree and basil
In the foothills of Macedonia:
A shepherd's crook on my shoulder

Hospital

Walking through the wards last night
I was trapped as if in a vial of
Poison

Slowly killed by bubbles
And drips
Of mumbles and buzzers and nurses
Bent over notes punched into keyboards:
Holding my breath over the stench of vomit and
Shit

White corridors seemed to snake for miles
Like coils of guts leading to final foul resting places
Of abandoned blaring televisions and
Plastic porridge bowls

This is no Asklepion:
There is no cypress tree or sea in sight:
And the mineral springs have made way
For a lukewarm stream that chills
Her feet and races toward the dirty drain

Memories

She sits quietly under grey clouds
Heavy with thoughts which scatter
Like the wavy lines of cirrus above:

Bars of time
Imprison her mind
Wading between the tangles of tomato and rosemary
And wrinkled mint

Muddling our names
And faces we giggle
With grief

'What month were you born?'
My mother asks
And watches me through squinting eyes

Memories of my baby clothes drying
Under that forty-year November sun
Long vanished from her mind

Patient

The starched drapes hide me like an unwilling
Actor trembling in the wings
An upturned cockroach trapped in a horizontal bottle
Whilst the doctors argue amongst themselves about falling
instruments
And spilled medicine

And tell me not to yell
As the needle moves through my spine
Like a loaded submarine

Watching the baby rise and fall inside me like a demon
My belly lifting like a fleshy balloon on the table
They giggle and point like schoolchildren
With plastic stethoscopes
And too big coats

And as the surgeon's brush weeps salty iodine over my stomach
Painting my belly like a fat brown lip
Which the scalpel turns red
It strikes me that his bare skinny legs
Are as pink as musk sticks
In his boyish shorts

Drained like a pond the flapping bald fish falls into my hands
Its pink gums hooking on breast
And the orderly who comes to wheel me away
Stands transfixed without shame
Evaluating the catheter between my legs
Which traps me to the bed

Fishing

We goaded the fat trout
With brown confetti
And the promise of more
Thrown into the lake with a twist of the wrist

The most sensitive ones are
Caught I suppose:

Their jaw aching with hook

As they lash head and tail
Leaving a veil of red
In the wide white bucket

That trout must have had a poetic soul:
Since it wanted to see and suffer
And yearn for what lay beyond the depths

Its gills opened and closed
Violently drinking the air:
And the flesh was as white and sweet
As Arabian jasmine

The Hill Range

When the hill range was younger
I would sit on the balcony
Admiring the woven green belt
Which snaked past tractors
And Olympus' milky head

Holding the metal of the balcony
I would slip a leg through the bars
Laughing as my slipper fell below
Sometimes on the soil
Or a passerby's head

And by evening the sunset's saffron threads
Would fall beyond the fields
Of cotton and olive
With their white and black baubles
Ready to be picked off the green
By fingers scratched and worn

I had hoped to catch some of the warmth on my head:
And a little sandy soil
In my shoe

The City

I passed like an ant
Through the city tonight
Crawling through the dark alleys

How it's changed
This old town:

Through ice-cream and balloon
Long ago
The roads once seemed wider and filled with promise

But tonight it was caked with sleaze
And despair
Its flashing lights and
Garish signs loomed above me
Like a boorish man pressed too close

His fat gold watch
Ticking in my ear

The Parkville Embassy
Post Natal

The embassy folded its flag
Long ago

And became a boarding house
For the stateless ones:
Bloated men with hollow eyes
Their arms tacked with tracks

There seemed to be many visitors in dark glasses
And strange cars at all hours of the day
The windows always ablaze at midnight
Like unsleeping eyes
Watching me even as I stood leaning
With the dizziness of pregnancy
Gulping the cold air in my stretched skin

And where polite conversations were once had
In the rooms with
High ceilings and elegant fireplaces:
The grand entrance now stank of cigarettes
Profanity and urine
And vodka bottles stained the balcony
Like clear gargoyles

I would steer the pram away quickly:
Even though I was drawn to visit
The Edwardian dame

With her bent wrought-iron veranda:

Decline was something I understood
When the jabot had made way for the pram

Its wheels would clatter
Like crazed tongues on the cobbles
Towards colourful rosellas which roosted
Above my screaming head
Past the buzzing powerlines and the ding
Of the number 57 tram

Date

The winter wind wheezes like an old man;
And my spade struggles to meet
The cold head of earth as it
Lies bald
Pale and freezer-licked
The bare toes and fingers of trees
Poking through the rain

Will it do to plant
That precious date seed
Still warm with the sugar
And sun of the East?

Delicious pearl of the desert
You remind me of something

Or perhaps someone:

A proud palm amongst the bare winter sticks
As unlikely as laugher in the grave

The Fig Tree

The fig tree hangs bent
In summer's flushed face:
A woody Quasimodo
Balanced on ancient rocks

Mesmerized
Though my hands are soft
And inked
Ancestors reach through me
With earthy cracked arms:
Branches as worn as a peasant's
Finger

I wring the fruit from the neck;
And expertly pull the tender green bell towards
Me

The milk from its bleed
Burns my pale hand
And opens the skin like a mouth

Alone

I took the end row seat;
Petulant and fickle
A distant planet
Flung far from its axis

Sitting silent and stern:
A suited staring cat
Taking in the twang and twist of unearthly violin

The solivagant flute played
Doleful tunes under lights
As stark as ice moons

And I chained my arms around my body
As I watched the concert
For I was afraid that if I released my sides
I would disintegrate into dust
And be flung into the darkness of space

The man next to me sits by himself also:
With all the world shimmering in his hand
Smiling in the dark
At his lover's text

Tongue

It's hard to address
Someone like you;

I stand dumb and my tongue
Is a velvet sash
Hanging limp
And soundless

Is it enough to
Dip my pen
Into the ink of your eyes:
Black as cuttlefish

And let my soul speak
Unfurling like cotton:
Weaving poetry
Instead?

Life

How can it be:

That a dying heart
Gallops fastest
At daybreak's blush

And that eyes dark
With death
See the light?

The rough gravel of that road
Pierced my shoe like a thousand silver bullets:
Rocks travelled upwards to become my
Mouth and eyes
Becoming the path
Through which others may tread:
Coming to rest like wild dandelions
At my shoulder

Foreigner in the Village

We were an out-blowing of hopes
Swaddled in home-sewn clothes and tacked on boats
Cleared by indifferent doctors
Pointing ahead
With their nicotine-stained fingers

The cheeks of nostalgia
Blew us back
And I hoped I was invisible
Under cloak of foreign passport and
Word and dress

I tried to hide my broad hands
In too-tight gloves
But every rock spelled my name
And the trees seemed to whisper
In my ear:
As I recognized the school on the hill
Whose schoolrooms I had never met

Windows creaked open
Their paint flaking under ruby sun
And the people stared in recognition
Trapping me under their heavy eye

Parthenon

Today we have dressed ourselves smartly
The children and I
Flitting in amongst the Athenian rabble
Of cameras and touts and souvenirs
Which clatter and snap like bouncing
Dice on boards

We will pay our respects
To our broken grandfather
High on the rock:
Panting we reach the top stepping
Gingerly through marble; our bony legs weave
Through rocks and clefts where wildflowers spring
Our feet and neck salty with effort

His bones
Stand splintered and yellow;
Blasted and stripped by gunpowder
And chisel
The early morning sun sprints
Through columns and friezes and we stand agape
Quietly
Hands folded like paper purses and our pupils and phones
filling with
History

Catching our breath like
Sated mountain goats
Nostrils filling with sage and the fumes
Of morning traffic

Trees

Why won't let my lemon tree grow?
The soil is clay-hard and unwelcoming under the
Californian bungalow:
Unfertilized by braying donkeys it sits like a perfect
Smooth stick
Shaking its bony limbs under the perch of magpies
Wasp-filled swellings on mottled wood bulging like
Silent Trojans

Yet how sensuously the florets of the pomegranate fall
Redolent of sun and sleep in my mother's village:
The thyme – kissed bees flitting in and out
Of golden dots like devoted lovers
I tease them by shaking
The branch
Letting their yellow-smeared noses
Brush my arm briefly with the dust of spring

Perhaps some of it will travel with me on my journey
To my grey home
Rubbing off accidentally on my clothes
And I will pollinate the garden like a
Giant bee

My pockets fill with lemons from a tree
As tall as an Ottoman mansion:
I smell and bite them
Hoping for a scratch of gold
Under my nail

Father's Home

I search for my father's home
But my hands and mind cannot follow lines on maps
So I cock my ear and listen to the
Scream of the wind here on this mountain
Instead

It carries my father's boyish laugh
And my mother's blush
Their love song ringing through fruited groves

Their voices move my feet like compass arrows
Leading me to that whitewashed hut
As broken as a tooth
And my heart flies like a pigeon towards its nest
Though the door is closed
And the window lifts slightly at the noise outside:

An old man's ear posted to the curtain

Loneliness

The house seems bigger
Somehow:
Echoes wail
Between grey walls

Curtains hang
Drooped and drawn
And hail scatters on the tiles
Like tumbling rice
Falling in my ears
Swirling
Like daggers of ice

I gorge the sounds hungrily
And my mind bloats and blocks
Like a sparrow's stomach

The Mirror

The mirror stands clubfooted
In the spare room:
Bent slightly forward in her mahogany frame
Watching me with a quiet eye

Our heads come together:
Grandmother mirror and I
Much she has witnessed:
Both the writhing and moan
Of love and grief
Saving secrets beneath her passive
Face
Still and dusty
Her eyes as shiny as a girl's

The Wind

What is the purpose of the wind
But to whisper its poetry
To the tree?

Look at how its leaves shake with emotion
When the wind embraces it!

Winding through cobblestones
Spring roses
And feverish brows
It cries and laughs
At all it hears

How drawn I am to the smell of a freshly cut book:
Holding it close to my nose
Like a newborn baby
It must be the breath of wind echoing
Through page and print

Unicorn

Night entered
The heart of day like a
Cloaked thief
His dagger hidden from our sun
As we rode on the edge of
A golden world
The spokes of our wheels spinning
In harmony

Until they split:
Those bleeding chambers
Stabbed on the horn of a unicorn
Which waited quietly on our track

Photograph

An old sepia photograph
Trapped between glue and plastic
And thin sheets
Holds the toughest man I know:

His cheekbones sharp as razors
Jutting like sea-washed rocks
Below lighthouse eyes
Which shone and scanned
Looking for danger

And the same unsmiling mouth
Which I later came to know:
The lips curled like a sea snake's
So much younger of course:
Less crumpled by the tides of Poseidon's pool
Which bathed him in salt
And cured his tongue

Tongues

When she tired of the endless verbal arrows
The curses and quarrels
She would retreat into her fortress
Of stove and pan

Casting the ox's tongues into the boil

Sliding them
On the chopping board
Their buds skinned by a flick of her knife
They fell like bloated soundless men
Into moats of vinegar and salt
Served with just the right amounts of silence

We sat on stools of dagger
And chewed on bitter food
Which made a hole in our stomach
Too big to fill

Mines

The script of our life was forged
In a copper mine
Their picks and eyes
Colliding between rock and sand

Choked with ash they came to
The surface
As blind as rats

Their arms conditioned to chip
And crack even in the sun
And the black lung
Of the hearth

Vase

I found the vase in the exact way
I found you:

In the midst of everyday chatter
Somewhere in the far end of the room:
Delicate like porcelain or maybe glass:
With two arms delicately entwined
On either side
Eyes and frown exquisitely painted
As by the stroke of a silky brush

Quickly inspected
With the eye of a collector
And mine for the taking

Over the mantelpiece it now sits silently

That vase:

Its face lined by the heat of the fireplace
Arms glossless and lightly gathering dust:
Beautiful
And redundant

Bread

My grandmother lies trapped under
The glass of the picture frame
Wearing a kerchief tightly around her head
Turkish style

Her strong hands flecked with dough
And the brown of an oven's spit
The paddle of the loaf's shovel which entered the
Fire like a tongue stands smouldering
And black
Next to her and my grandfather

Her bread always tasted of salt

Or tears

And the crust was grainy
Like finely crushed bone

The Wall

I can't see the crack
In the wall tonight –

Usually it lets in a little light
Or a flicker of moon

But the mud and cement
And tufts of neglect
Have covered its eye
Insurmountable
And grey

Standing in Goliath's shadow

Dirt and rock and sling
Shift from my hand
To my mouth

Results

I imagine it was as grey as cloud
Sitting grumpily in the kidney dish
Slightly deflated
By the slashing thunderbolt
Of the surgeon's knife

Thumbing through pathology results
Like shell-shocked soldiers fingering maps
We track the aggressor on paper
Classed into size and spread

Her left side was pruned
Red with signs of enemy track
And tied with stitches of steel

Our eyes dart like flying geese
Silent chins in hand and our boots
Still and muddy

Camouflage

In between the zebra lines
Of encyclopaedia
And
Poem
I hid like ducking prey
Quietly
In school libraries
Pockets filled with
Dismay

Quietly burying myself in between
Its camouflage
And finding allies
In undulating stripes
Of rhyme and loop

While my mates grappled with
Grenades of sex and smokes
I observed them with envy
Through the jungle green
My jowls as empty as a dead cat's

Artist's Underworld

We had entered the dark bowels
Of the theatre
My brother and I;
Ushered in by a pimply faced
Cerberus
Protecting his domain as fiercely
As any guard dog

I sat glued
Like a frog to glass
Watching her dance:
Plié and pirouette
As pale as Isadora

The ticket softened with sweat in my pocket
As her silk slippers and stubbed toes
Bled in the shadowy underworld of art

The Mulberry Tree

Bury me under the mulberry

He said

Where the inky birds dot paper skies
And the grate of sighs and sobs
Is silenced by the shake of emerald crowns
And plump water drops will fall
Into my open mouth

Let me nestle in the arms
Of its strong roots in
Blankets of dark silk
Spun by the mouths of silkworms

The Vineyard

Nothing was missing on that late spring day:
The children's tongues buzzed like bees
On the light-filled bus
Jokes and yelps dripping like honey
On the combs of our ears

And the vineyards of the valley
Were covered in white nets
Cast over young bodies by farmers
Unwilling to share:
Red and green eyes
Hiding like covered brides;
Or beekeepers in white suits
Casting sleep with
Lanterns of smoke

The vine leaves are open and green
Like the hand of Fatima
Their veins plump with the juice
Of mirth and slumber

The Poet

Frenetic in her waxy mausoleum
Bridging gaps between dark
And light
The poet becomes a worker bee
Dancing behind stripes and cells
Gathering pollen of eyes and smiles
Her mouth pours word

And every poem is a sting
Which tears her belly:
She bleeds
And leaves her mark with honey

War

The greatest war we fight
Is love:
A catapult of the mouth
A spear of cold eye
And how our blood runs;

Hot with pain

And yet we yearn for the battle
And turn knowingly toward the fire

Drop the breastplate and greaves:
To be naked
Is the greatest measure of strength

Sounds

The voice of a nightingale
Ribbons through the dark
Of dusk and dawn
Curious in the quiet

Pipes and warbles
It seems
Are formed in crucibles of darkness

Stillness as large as elephant's ears

And as beautiful as the scratch
Of an uncapped pen

Yearning

The yoke of yearning leaned heavily on my
Glass shoulders;

A torturous beam causing crack and chip as
I lay down like a gopher
Beaten flat
My dirt-filled nose burrowing:

Searching for that voice
And face
Somewhere in the black earth of youth
And my comfortless bed

Constellations in Ancient Skies

Usurper of day:
A sardine-silver moon
Arching and curving in the net
Of dark

Its light-filled scales dot Andromeda's mouth:
Starbursts read by ancient hands
Blindly feeling in the dark
Chiton-dressed star sailors trace heaven's braille
Until the cry of lark

Traveller

You:

The veteran of so many wrecks
A face lined by salt and sun
As chipped as Gibraltar

Eyes forever turned to the distance
Always seeking shores
And white doves clenching branches of olive

Traveller:

Is there a difference between the Atlantic
And your tear?
Equal in amount of salt:
Both sing of journeys into the
Deep

Lift

Just for a short moment
Our bodies feel lighter after lifting
A burden

Have you ever felt it?

It is almost as if arm
Or spine
Have become wing floating skyward
Catching the grey beard of a wise man
Or a cloud

And yet how we fear the weight
And measure and squabble over each gram
Like a miser who counts each coin
And throws them quickly
Like dead birds
Into his moth-eaten pocket

Melbourne May 2020

When the cacophony of coins
And cars and trains hushed
The river gurgled a little louder
Like a baby free of swaddling cloth:

The bones of the gumtrees
Creaked and waved

Like stooped elders bent
To the ground and spun
With shade
Stiff green fingers pointing
Arthritically at my head

Sighing with the joy of a toothless crone
Whose suitor has arrived
Much too late

Village Blanket

This blanket once hung on a wooden loom:
As red as a pomegranate
Its threads of wool combed from grandfather's sheep
And dyed blood red in the boiling pot

The whole frame must have shuddered in her little hand
Like a birthing woman
As she passed the shuttle between warp and weft
Working under lamp
The threads twisting like umbilical cords
As it slowly shaped over days
And months becoming full in her hand

It is starting to fray a little at the corners
For its journey has been as long as the fold
And the boys tell me it is too small for their bed:

One day I will tell them to lay their heads on it
And quietly listen for the scratch of the olive
And the warmth of her hand

Chalice Drum

He drew across the chalice drum
Dragging his fingers
Like camels draw their feet in sand

Speaking of Rumi and Hafiz:
Each finger stroking
As if it were over the swollen belly
Of a lover

What harmony between man and music!

His face as flushed as oven pebbles
Music flowing from his hands
Like Elburz streams

Telescope

My eye was always on the wrong side
Of the telescope:

Seeking the diamond eye of the star
In the soundless loom of space
With its shattered glass
Which litters the sky like a madman's cup:

How I searched for meaning amongst splinters
And for understanding in that grey, silent face
Rocket marked
As it stared at me nightly
Dead-eyed through my window

Should the earth not have been enough?

I should have slathered my skin with dirt
Alive with pulse and ray and beast

Yet it seemed impossible
Whilst I still had hands

Loner

He passes me daily in his thin yellow coat;
Always unchanged and a little abrupt with
His loud shoes and silent lip –
That mysterious loner
A loping camel lashed by
Sand in his loveless eye
His soul scorched and
Burnt like desert sun

As much as he resists his feet must rest a while;
Peeled as they are from the heat of effort
He seeks a tree on this grey-black city road:
To stand under it for a moment
And feel the shade
Of frond and fruit

Rush Hour

Watching from the platform
Trains hiss and glint under morning rays
Those long grey serpents
Racing
Like shot poison
Through vein tracks

Worn briefcases and laddered stockings
We shatter and spread blindly forward
Into the city's heart
Briefcases lodged on the sharp horizons
Of Eureka and Rialto

And in the station's mirror I gaze
Into eyes as green as venom

Thessaloniki Promenade

The city murmurs with the life of
An aestival breeze which rushes over
The bay's spinach-coloured lamps

Just a stone's throw from Freedom Square:

Where the Nazis collected passengers
For the cattle wagon and
Paved the streets with gravestones
Plucked from the arms of the dead

And the port is covered in tourist junks
Last seen in Vietnam:
Burnt corn cobs and flying metal umbrellas
And the statue of a sworded Alexander:
Covered by the blown bubbles
Of immigrants
Armed with their plastic wands and empty hats

The Tower on the corner is a stern sentinel
White-washed to cover the blood of Greeks
A proud grandfather with windows like everywhere eyes:
And I climb inside his belly
Through the winding stair
Up towards the turrets and gape
At a girl pointing her naked legs upward
In a handstand her dress and top falling
Like broken colourful petals
Toward the stirring City below

Icon

That silent eye of judgement
Seems to be the mark of saints:
Bathed in the oil of icons
And blurry because of it

I have bent the nail and
Lifted the wood clean off the walls:
A reverse guillotine

Heavy as it is with incense
And as dark as the flocks of heads
Silent below it

And through the hole I see
The church
Of tree and sky
And the great tattered robe
Which floats on the stream

A single severed finger
Resting on the cape

Dreams

How cruel dreams can be:
Those nightly reels spun on memories and trouble

A face, half-forgotten,
Alights in the circle of my dozing eye
Smiles of long ago
As vivid as broken roses on the breeze

Only to evaporate
Like passing ghosts taking leave
From dusty attics
Leaving us to grapple with the memory
In our dark beds

Asylum Seeker

If you knew me you would know
That waves are as
Loud as the crack of a gun

Briny whips have wiped my name
From my mouth:
I am a boat number
A pair of sewn lips
A salty vessel

How beautiful my poetry will be
Once it has fermented in the darkness
Like a loaf or wine
My words will be dark birds flocking
And flying like burnt ribbons
Leaving ash in the heart

But first:

Let me embrace my son
Who clings to my dry breast:
Now that I have rescued him from the cold
And thrown him into the fires of hell

My arms enclose him
In a prison of our own:
Salty tears and the cruel splash of ocean
Taste the same

Rhodes July 1944

Giant muscat grapes hang limply like slaughtered rabbits
Over baking walls
Their dull liquorice eyes as silent
As the dusty streets

Where are the children
With their plaits and books
And woollen pants?
Neatly written names have been called
In tones as righteous as a school master's
From a book bound in rich red leather

And the boats have come to rock them to sleep
In their cold hands
The tap of their engines spreading metallic dirges
Like backward lullabies
Over minaret and turret and bundles of bitter oregano
Growing on the silent steps

Days

This morning I watched the burning cheek of sun
Dragged across the sky
And let it bleed on my face:

So few are the mornings which are left
That I could have kicked myself
For preferring the darkness and still
Of sleep-numbed lips

I should have reached for those orange and red celestial reins
And tipped the gold chariot filled with melted trumpets
On my shoulder
As I slip into the dark

Even the winters that I dreaded
Now glow in my hands like
Melting fractals of light:
And I gather morning mists and fallen feathers
In mind's pocket like a hoarder

Cyprus – Ancient Kourion

Bent towards the sun and sea
Like a widow
The tree watches the wind breathe through the site
With its hanging olive eyes
Teasing past earthquake-rocked porticos and
Empty baths

Conquerors arrive in buses these days:
Resting under her shadow like sun stunned beasts
Chewing loudly from plastic lunchboxes
Fingers pointed at reconstructed theatres

Reading of Hellenikos
And Margaritis in glossy brochures
They turn and sniff the air for tea
And proclaim they can go no further
Their mosquito-bitten legs as thick
As broken columns

And the tree sheds her bitter fruit
Spilling black on cracked marbles

As a dog-eared entrance ticket
Lies flat under their flimsy sandles

A Thousand Cranes

How many hopes and dreams
Have sailed
And foundered
On the white wings of sea?

Those waves carry salt-filled gasps of dream
Their sharp breath hitting me like a midwife's hand
Filling my lungs with air
They fold sharp into rocks,
Journeys with foamy noses
Crashing and forming
Like a thousand paper cranes

Flying

Today the woman is flying
On a stretcher pulled by young people
Their pale faces unlined with burden

A broken Icarus swallowed by
The metallic mouth of the ambulance
Waving to the children
In their perfect clothes

Her leg points away from her body
And house
And it is time to leave:
The ankle has snapped like a sunflower's neck
Pointing west like a spent weathervane
Spun dizzy
Lying sprawled like a fast-breathing mare on the wet steps
Which she has swept and polished
And bleached on better days

She flies again later
Held down by six pairs of hands
Paralysed
In the dark alleys of hallucination
Hovering over the well-worn feet
And hands

Hold on while we put your leg back in
She hears them say while she rests

And she wonders if she ever fitted anyway

And if the leg:

Worshipped by doctor and nurse on the altar of ketamine
Has broken under the burden
Of keeping her whole

Orthopedic Ward

They wheel her in a little after midnight
A mosaic on a trolley
The pale curtains fluttering like white moths with the force of
Her bellows and the push
Of the starched bed
A dark dreamcatcher on plastic rings

Sometime during the night
The rest of us moan too
Swaddled on beds in a nursery of splints
And useless shoes
Like arrested white ferries
In swelling water

And when morning snaps through the
Dirty window
We see each other for the first time
Though the voice is more familiar than the face

Pain Sisters

I say

And we laugh

And for the first time I begin to hate the colour white:

The gauze and consent form:

The flash of the nurse's torch

The choke of evening pills

And the white broken bones which
Grind and rattle like the cries of a bride
Whose too-white bridal sheets
Have forced her back
To her father's home

MARIA PAPAGEORGIOU FOROUDI was born in Melbourne in 1979 to immigrant parents. She is a lawyer who practises in community law and is passionate about the environment and social justice. Her writing explores various themes related to family, heritage, journeys and womanhood. Published in *Inscape* (1997) and *Antipodes Periodical*, she has won prizes and commendations for her poetry and short stories in the Greek Australian Cultural League's Literary Competition, 2005, 2006, 2015 and 2017, and was published in UK Anthology *VSS 365-Volume One: A Series of Stunning Very Short Stories from Around the Globe* in 2019. She is married and lives in Melbourne with her husband and two sons.

Many of the poems in this collection first appeared as part of the vss365 prompt on Twitter. The author is indebted to members of Twitter's writing community for their support.

.

www.ingramcontent.com/pod-product-compliance
Ingram Content Group Australia Pty Ltd
76 Discovery Rd, Dandenong South VIC 3175, AU
AUHW020841060325
407965AU00004B/44